The Cape of Rushes

Antonia Barber

Illustrated by Amanda Harvey

CAMBRIDGE
UNIVERSITY PRESS

There was once a rich man with three beautiful daughters, all of whom loved their father dearly. The rich man held a feast to celebrate his birthday, inviting his friends from far and near.

By nightfall, he had eaten too much of the good food and drunk too deeply of the fine red wine. Greedy for praise, he told each of his daughters to stand up in turn and to tell the company how much she loved him.

"Father," said the eldest, "I love you as I love my life!"
The guests applauded and the rich man was pleased.

4

"Father," said the second, "I love you more than anything in the world!" The guests cheered and the rich man was delighted.

Then he turned to his third daughter, who sat with her
eyes cast down. "Speak up!" he said.

The youngest daughter looked up at him and smiled. "Why,
Father," she said, "I love you as fresh meat loves salt."

Her answer sent a ripple of laughter around the table,

but her father frowned. He was quick to anger and the red wine had made him foolish. "As fresh meat loves salt! That is no love at all," he roared. "I will not give food and shelter to an ungrateful child." And though her sisters pleaded, he drove the girl from his house, telling her never to return.

Alone in the dark night, she shivered in her fine silk dress until the rising moon showed that her path was fringed with beds of rushes. These she gathered as she went and, with nimble fingers, wove a long cape to cover her dress from top to toe.

It was as well that she did, for soon the rain began to fall. Her lovely hair grew bedraggled and her dainty shoes grew muddy, but, beneath the cape of rushes, her white dress stayed clean and dry.

Many miles she walked. She came at last to a fine mansion
with lighted windows gleaming against the darkness. She
knocked at the kitchen door and the cook opened it.

"Do you need a maid?" asked the girl hopefully.

"We have servants enough," replied the cook.

"I will work hard," said the girl. "Only give me a dry
corner and a little food."

The cook felt sorry for her. "Will you scrape pots and scrub pans?" she asked.

"Willingly," said the girl.

So the cook took her in and gave her all the worst jobs which the other servants hated. The girl would tell no-one her name, so they called her 'Cape-of-Rushes'. In time it seemed to her that she had no other name.

Her only joy as she moved about the house was to catch sight of her new master's son. He was a good-hearted and handsome young man, and before long she was deeply in love. But he hardly noticed her as she passed in the shadows, hidden beneath her cape of rushes.

Midwinter came and the season of goodwill when the master
of the house welcomed his neighbours. There were feasts and
dances, and the servants were allowed to watch from a doorway.
But, for the girl in the cape of rushes, the sight of her love in
the arms of another was more than she could bear.

Silently she crept away to the scullery. Alone and unseen, she washed her face, cleaned her dainty shoes, put up her hair and took off the cape of rushes. Then she joined the dancers in her fine silk dress and no-one there knew who she was.

The master's son was enchanted by this lovely girl, fairer
and more richly dressed than all the rest. Through the long,
bright evening, he would dance with no other. But, before the
ball was over, she slipped away from him. Back in the scullery,
she took down her hair and put on the cape of rushes before
the other servants returned.

Next day, the kitchen fairly buzzed with excitement as the maids talked of the lovely girl who had cast a spell upon their young master.

"I wish I had seen her," said the girl in the cape of rushes.

"Watch with us tonight," said the others. "There is another ball and she may come again."

But instead she hid herself away, took off her cape of rushes, pinned up her hair and joined the dancing.

The young man smiled as she entered the ballroom. He took her in his arms and would not let her go. He seemed afraid to take his eyes off her, for fear that she would vanish as she had done before. But as the night drew to a close, she slipped away again. Letting down her hair, she hid her white dress beneath the cape of rushes.

A week passed before the next ball, which marked the end of the festive season. Once more the cape of rushes was thrown down and the shining hair pinned up. Once more the youngest daughter entered the brightly lit ballroom to dance with the man she loved.

His heart beat fast at the sight of her. All week he had dreamed of her, afraid that she would not come again.

All night he danced with her and sought to find out her name. When she would not tell it, he gave her his ring saying, "You are my only love and unless you will be mine, I shall die."

Yet still she slipped away, back to the cold, damp scullery and, taking down her hair, covered her brightness with the dull cape of rushes.

Then the festive house became a house of sadness, for the master's son fell sick. Messengers were sent every way in search of the girl who had stolen his heart, but no trace could be found of her. The young man could neither sleep nor eat, so deep was his grief.

The cook came down to the kitchen with orders to make
a tasty broth which might tempt him to eat a little.

"Let me make it for you," said the girl. When it was done,
she dropped the ring into the bowl.

The cook took it to the young man, who drank it listlessly until he spied the ring at the bottom. "Who made the broth?" he asked.

"Why . . . I did," lied the cook, afraid that she might find herself in trouble.

"No," said the young man gently. "You must tell me the truth, for my life depends upon it."

"Well, then," said the cook, "it was the maid in the cape of rushes."

"Send her to me," said he.

The girl came in, downcast and dull in her cape of rushes.
"Did you make my broth?" asked the young man.
"I did," she said, and he heard the voice he loved.
"Where did you get the ring?" he asked her.
"From him who gave it to me." As she spoke, she raised
her head and he gazed into the eyes he loved.

"Who are you?" breathed the young man.

"I will show you," she said. Smiling, she let fall the cape of rushes and stood before him in her white silk dress, glistening with pearls and silver thread. Then he knew that he had found the girl he loved.

At once, the master's son grew well again, and soon they were to be married. It was to be a grand wedding, more splendid than any of the balls. Guests were invited from near and far, and the youngest daughter found that her father and her sisters would be among them. And still she had told no-one her true name.

As the wedding feast was being prepared, the girl went
down to the kitchen.

"Dear Cook," she said, "I want you to cook all the meats
without adding any salt."

"Without salt?" said the cook in horror. "But, my lady,
if I do they will have no flavour!"

"I know it," said the girl. "Nevertheless, do as I ask you."

The wedding day came and the young couple were married amid great rejoicing.

When the ceremony was over, the bride would not take off her wedding veil, not even for the wedding feast.

The banquet looked splendid, but when the guests tried the meats, they were so dull and tasteless that it was hard to eat them.

The girl's father tasted first one and then the others. At last, to everyone's astonishment, he gave a great cry of despair.

"Why, sir, what is wrong?" asked the master of the house.

"My lord," said the father, "I once had a third daughter. I asked her how much she loved me and she answered, 'As fresh meat loves salt.' Now I understand her meaning, for without salt the meat is worthless. But then I thought her cold and unloving; I drove my daughter from my house, and now I fear that I may never see her face again."

As he spoke, the bride rose from her place and came to
where he sat. She put up her bridal veil and said, "Father,
she stands before you."

Then father and daughter wept for joy in each other's arms
and her sisters greeted her with loving kisses. The bridegroom
was glad to see his bride restored to riches and honour; but
in his heart she remained for ever the young maid in the cape
of rushes.